DECO LAndmarks

RICHFIELD BUILDING, LOS ANGELES, CALIFORNIA   LA18

DECO LAndmarks
ART DECO GEMS OF LOS ANGELES

BY ARNOLD SCHWARTZMAN ⚹ FOREWORD BY BEVIS HILLIER

CHRONICLE BOOKS
SAN FRANCISCO

FRONT COVER:
Bronze panel above
the main entrance of the
Times Mirror Building,
1931–35.
Los Angeles.

BACK COVER:
Los Angeles City Hall,
1928.
Los Angeles.

ENDPAPERS:
Cast stone bas-relief
fire escape,
Hollywood–Western
Building, 1928.
Los Angeles.

PAGE 1:
Sheet metal frieze,
Grandstand facade,
Santa Anita Racetrack,
1935.
Arcadia.

PAGE 2:
Postcard,
PAGE 3:
Detail, bronze
elevator doors,
AND OPPOSITE:
Plan of front elevation,
Richfield Oil Building,
1929, demolished in 1968.
Los Angeles.

Library of Congress Cataloging-in-Publication
Data available.

ISBN 0-8118-4601-6

Manufactured in China.

Designed by Arnold & Isolde Schwartzman

Distributed in Canada by Raincoast Books
9050 Shaughnessy Street
Vancouver, British Columbia V6P 6E5

10 9 8 7 6 5 4 3 2 1

Chronicle Books LLC
85 Second Street
San Francisco, California 94105

www.chroniclebooks.com

ACKNOWLEDGMENTS

With grateful thanks to the following for
their generous assistance:
Robert S. Birchard
Hollywood Heritage Inc.
Los Angeles Conservancy
Gloria Miller, Debbie Stone, and
   Gene Strauss, Fox Studios
Travis Montgomery, The Queen Mary
Robert W. Nudelman
Fran Offenhauser
Barbara Smith, American Cinematheque
Kay Tornborg
Marc Wanamaker
Michael Webb

Very special thanks to my wife, Isolde,
for her assistance and dedication to the
production of this book.

Sincere gratitude to Bevis Hillier, the author
of the term "Art Deco," for contributing the
foreword to this book.

CONTENTS

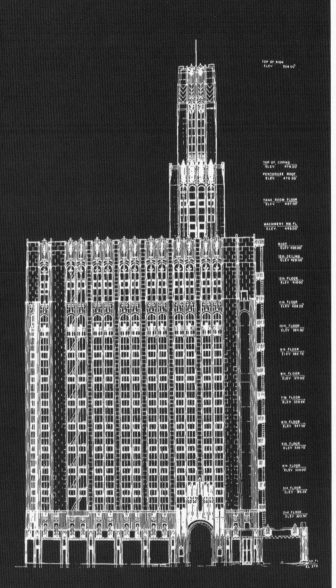

FOREWORD

In 1983, as part of my research for a biography of Sir John Betjeman, the British Poet Laureate, I spent a month at the Huntington Library in San Marino, California. After two weeks I had finished my work and had some time on my hands.

I wrote to the editor of the *Los Angeles Times* asking whether the paper would be interested in an article about the city. At the same time I inquired about the possibility of a staff position. I was invited to lunch in the boardroom, with a cadre of senior staff, including Jean Sharley Taylor, the top-ranking woman at the *Times*, and the genial arts editor Charles Champlin. It was, I realized, a sort of informal interview. At the end of lunch, Champlin handed me an envelope. "This may be mission impossible," he said with a grin. The letter inside commissioned me to write two articles about L.A. — from an outsider's point of view.

I already had some experience of the city. I had first come to L.A. in 1973, as editor of *The Connoisseur* magazine, and explored the city — especially the magnificent, aero-dynamic Pan Pacific Auditorium of 1935. But when Chuck Champlin set my assignment ten years later, I still had a lot of legwork to do. I booked myself on bus tours of the city and read books, from Reyner Banham's *Los Angeles: A City of Four Ecologies* (whose 1971 edition had David Hockney's "A Bigger Splash" on its jacket) to the more detailed architectural survey by David Gebhard and Robert Winter from 1965.

In the first piece, I contrasted L.A. with San Francisco, which I had also visited for *The Connoisseur*. To me, San Francisco seemed a great European-style city of the belle époque, though much of it was built after the terrible earthquake and fire of 1906.

By contrast, L.A. was somehow definitively American, despite that its exceptional buildings in the Art Deco style adapted that idiom from France. In its majestic skyscrapers and other architectural and ornamental expressions, Art Deco was the first style, historically, in which the country surpassed the rest of the world.

Jean Taylor and Champlin liked my articles and offered me a post on the paper as associate editor and columnist for its magazine. In March 1984 I joined the staff in the splendid 1935 building, itself a prime monument of Art Deco, and was encouraged to further familiarize myself with the city. As I did so, I became aware of the dilapidation into which some of the finest Deco buildings were falling. One of the first pieces I wrote for the magazine was headed:

"DECO IN DANGER: THE FUTURE OF THE PAST" (8 July 1984). I wrote:

> *A journalist should not lose his objectivity. . . . Causes are not helped by apoplectic overstatement. But when I see what the people of Los Angeles are allowing to happen to their historic architecture, I want to sit on Eagle Rock and howl like the Hound of the Baskervilles. Howl in despair, because it is the eleventh hour — or later — for many of these buildings. The riot-act must be read now. Even a week later could be too late for buildings vulnerable to arson, accident or galloping decay.*

I pointed out that the city was "hardly bristling with medieval castles or eighteenth-century mansions," so it was perverse to tear down the memorable and historic buildings it did have. I added:

> *The trouble is that most of the buildings are twentieth-century and do not belong to the restrained tradition that has conventionally been most admired. It is still difficult for those whose beau ideal of architecture is a Georgian brick box with gables to accept architectural statements far more positive and histrionic — for example, the grand splurge exoticism of Sid Grauman's Chinese Theater (1927). . . . we should not yearn for City Hall to be Independence Hall, or for the Pan Pacific Auditorium to be a New York brownstone or a white, weather-boarded New England house. Panache in art is as valid as demure restraint. It is how well it is managed that matters.*

I dwelt on all the Deco buildings that had already been demolished, particularly the black and gold Richfield Building, to which an entire book had been devoted. The essential message of my article was, *Why do you think tourists come to Los Angeles?* My frustration called to mind a cartoon in the British comic magazine *Punch*. It showed a tourist guide saying to a gaggle of tourists, "This is your hotel. It stands on the site of one of the buildings you have come here to see."

My efforts to raise awareness of these endangered treasures would ultimately take a disappointing turn. In the *Times* article in that Orwellian — and L.A. Olympian — year 1984, I wrote that the Pan Pacific Auditorium was "still standing after several fires but in the last stages of picturesque decrepitude. It is perhaps the most imaginative 'streamline moderne' building in the world. There is still some talk of turning it into a hotel, and I would like to be optimistic."

A few days after the article appeared, I received a smarmy letter from Ed Edelman, supervisor of the city's Third District, who was responsible for the building's welfare. He assured me that he and his team had every intention of restoring the building. What made me doubt this very much was that earth-moving equipment had already done damage to outlying "architectural accessories" of the Pan Pacific. The Third District's total lack of concern for these suggested to me that it was hell-bent, for economic or political reasons, on turning the whole area into a park, and that it would not be in the least sorry if the auditorium went to blazes.

THE TIMES BUILDING. LOS ANGELES, CALIFORNI

And that is what it literally did. Before I left L.A. in 1988, the building was covered with gangland graffiti. Not long after I had returned to England for good, a colleague at the *Times* sent me a clipping from the paper, showing the auditorium engulfed in flames from an arson attack.

On the credit side, many notable buildings have been preserved. It took years, but I know that L.A. now has "one of the strongest preservation communities in the country," not just for its Deco treasures, but for the other buildings most identified with the city: the commercial roadside architecture of the pop-modern style. The Wiltern Theater was beautifully restored. The public library, in extreme King Tut style, suffered two arson attempts, but it has survived them. The El Rey Theater on Wilshire Boulevard — which at one stage in the late 1980s was painted shocking pink and used as a parking lot for motorbikes — has regained something of its old splendor. The gold, cylindrical building of the May Co. — near the La Brea tar pits — has been renovated, as part of the L.A. County Museum. It dates, as I do, from 1940.

Some twenty years since this particular story began, I have just completed the John Betjeman biography. He was an expert on architecture as well as a poet, and it has been said of his writings on that subject: "He was always interested in the shellfish as well as the shell" — in other words, the folk who had lived in the buildings, not just the masonry, the dry stones.

T180

63838

When Arnold told me he was working on this book, I was eager to see what he had photographed. I am specially pleased that he shows us those terrazzo floors that often survive in L.A. when the buildings they once signaled from the sidewalk have been converted beyond recognition or destroyed. (How did Arnold get the filthy gobs of chewing gum off the sidewalk?) It is good to see the Bullocks Wilshire department store (now, I'm told, a law school), whose fountain-like tower I used to pass every day on my bus ride to work. I recognize many old friends among the bas-reliefs and statues, but Arnold's enthusiasm and diligence have also put on parade many delightful and sometimes inspiring aspects of Deco design that I either never saw or never noticed. The vivid details bring out — in some cases more than seventy years after they were created — one of the defining qualities of Art Deco: *it still looks modern.*

The five years I spent in L.A. were the last of my youth: I did not realize it then, but do now. The polychrome images that coil, curve, zigzag, and fountain in this book were parts of my then habitat. To see them unfold again is a rare treat. Like my distinguished contemporary, the May Co. building, I feel positively renovated.

—BEVIS HILLIER

INTRODUCTION

The publication of this book coincides with and celebrates the eightieth anniversary of the Exposition Internationale des Arts Décoratifs et Industriels Modernes, held in Paris in 1925. Dedicated to the modern decorative arts, it brought together myriad designs from around the world and attracted some 16 million visitors. The exposition's influence quickly spread across the world and had a particularly strong impact on the United States, notably expressed in skyscrapers such as New York's Chrysler and RCA buildings.

The show introduced a style that reflected the new machine age and embraced all forms of design — fashion, film, transportation, product design, and architecture — and drew from a cocktail of art movements, including Cubism, Fauvism, and Futurism, and from the archaeological discoveries of the time, most notably the unearthing of Tutankhamen's tomb in 1922. The style was characterized by motifs of leaping gazelles, zeppelins, and ziggurats; saxophones, seaplanes, and sunbursts; and lightning bolts, flora, and fountains on surfaces from facades to mantel ornaments. These elements permeated a spectrum of household objects, such as cocktail cabinets, refrigerators, radios, fabrics, and clothing. Their most visible manifestation was in architecture.

The renewed interest in this design movement is due in part to a major exhibition on the period mounted by London's Victoria & Albert Museum in 2003, which enjoyed enormous success the following year in the United States. Among the many defining objects on view was the preserved grand entrance to London's Strand Palace Hotel. As a child, I loved to run my hands along the hotel lobby's fluted, illuminated glass handrails when I visited the Strand with my father, who worked as a waiter just across the road at the famed Savoy Hotel. The Savoy and its theater (the home of Gilbert and Sullivan operas) are other prime examples of the style. Due to his work surroundings, my father gained a keen interest in the new style, which in turn rubbed off on me. I believe that my first exposure was through his beautifully decorated Art Deco–style copy of *The Savoy Cocktail Book*. Consequently I learned to recognize the look from an early age, although I was unable to distinguish between the numerous labels associated with the style, such as Jazz Moderne, Zigzag Moderne, and Streamline Moderne — streamlining being essentially an American invention of the 1930s that reflected the concept of speed.

OPPOSITE:
Black vitrolite and silvered metal, The Darkroom Photographic Store, 1935–38. 5370 Wilshire Boulevard, Los Angeles. Marcus P. Miller.

Bevis Hillier, British art critic and historian, cleverly coined the expression "Art Deco" in his 1968 book, *Art Deco of the Twenties and Thirties*. The all-encompassing term has become a convenient shorthand label referring to the look that began with the boom of the Jazz Age of the 1920s and persisted through the Great Depression of the 1930s.

After the onset of the Depression in America, President Franklin D. Roosevelt established the New Deal. Two of the programs, the Public Works Administration (PWA) and the Works Progress/Projects Administration (WPA), created in 1933 and 1935, respectively, aimed to generate employment and promote the economy at a time when as much as 30 percent of the country's workforce was unemployed. Many artisans and architects benefited from this scheme and became fully employed, producing some of the most outstanding examples of Art Deco design that remain to this day. The fruits of these efforts can be seen throughout the public architecture of Los Angeles County in the work of muralists such as Hugo Ballin and sculptors Bartolo Mako, Millard Sheets, and Lee Lawrie, who produced fine bas-reliefs and metal and glass sculptures for schools, post offices, public libraries, and other civic facilities.

I further attribute my strong affinity for the Art Deco period to the fact that I was born at its zenith, 1936. That year the ocean liner RMS *Queen Mary* and the *Hindenberg* airship made their maiden voyages to New York, and the films *Modern Times* by Charles Chaplin, H. G. Wells's *Things to Come*, and Busby Berkeley's *Hollywood Hotel*, with its signature tune "Hooray for Hollywood," were produced. From an early age I had an equally strong attraction to Hollywood and the movies. The pink and blue pastel-shaded pages of my father's autograph book (dated the year of my birth) are filled with the signatures of the many visiting Hollywood celebrities he had served at the Savoy. When back in Los Angeles, these stars would cruise in their Cord and Duesenberg automobiles from their Malibu beach homes along Sunset Boulevard on their way to work at the Hollywood studios. On occasion, they would catch the SuperChief train from the Union Passenger Terminal to make the several days' journey to New York, and often traveled on to Europe aboard the ocean liners *Normandie* and *Queen Mary*, or on the *Hindenberg*, with its tubular chrome furnishings and aluminum grand piano. One of the first cities to embrace this new decorative language was Los Angeles, not only in its movies but also in its architecture. Some credit for this is due to the influx of the European émigrés who brought their skills to Los Angeles and the Hollywood studios, where their interpretation of Art Deco perfectly suited the fantasy world they wished to create on film.

In 1978 I came to Los Angeles to work in the "dream factory." On my first free weekend I set out to visit the city's many legendary architectural shrines. I had learned that some of the world's greatest architects worked in Los Angeles during the Art Deco period. These visionaries utilized glass, terra-cotta, and terrazzo, aluminum, stainless steel, and reinforced concrete, as well as new materials including a variety of plastic compounds, which went under the trade names Bakelite, Catalin, and Formica. In the 1950s, many of the city's Art Deco architectural features were considered passé and were covered up. Today they are being uncovered and preserved — and newly appreciated.

Among my recent favorite discoveries are the terra-cotta-glazed Eastern Columbia building (pages 36/37); the terrazzo floor on the sidewalk outside Clifton's Cafeteria (pages 40/41/42); and Griffith Observatory (after major renovation due for completion in 2005, it will once again become a shining beacon atop Griffith Park). I became fascinated by the ship-like Coca-Cola Company building (page 64) and the equally nautical-styled Crossroads of the World complex in Hollywood (page 111), both designed by Robert V. Derrah — these two structures are among the finest examples of Streamline Moderne in Los Angeles (comparable to Welton Becket and Walter Wurdeman's Pan Pacific Auditorium, destroyed by fire in 1989). Further notable examples are Hollywood High School with its Bartolo bas-reliefs (page 113); the black vitreous facade of The Darkroom on Miracle Mile, resembling a 35 mm camera (page 10); and S. Charles Lee's Hollywood–Western Building (pages 102/103), its bas-relief fire escapes portraying the art of moviemaking. It is ironic that a building covered in nude figures should house the "Czar of all the rushes" — Will Hays, the MPPDA Censor, whose office was on the fourth floor! Lee's Academy cinema, now a cathedral, another extreme example of Streamline Moderne, is believed to have been built as the home of the Academy Awards; however, the Academy has no record of this. Other favorites include Grauman's Chinese and Egyptian Theaters and the downtown Mayan Theater for their exoticism (pages 57/58/59).

Surviving gems of note are the Union Passenger Terminal (page 110), which combines the Spanish and Streamline Moderne styles; the renovated Pantages (pages 106/107) and

Sidewalk terrazzo
floor medallion,
Clifton's Brookdale
Cafeteria, 1936.
648 S. Broadway,
Los Angeles.
Clifford Clifton.

Wiltern (pages 25/82/146) theaters; and the department stores
Bullocks Wilshire (pages 108/109), which has been termed
"Parisien Moderne" (now a law school), and the May Co. (page 32),
with its distinctive Streamline Moderne gold mosaic cylindrical
facade (now part of the Los Angeles County Museum of Art).
Even Max Factor has had a "makeover" — the elegant
pink and white marble Regency Moderne building is
now a movie museum (page 80).

On my bookshelves, nestled beside my
father's 1932 copy of *The Savoy Cocktail Book*,
is the Oscar that I received. This iconic symbol
of Hollywood and the Art Deco period was
sculpted in 1927 by George Stanley, who was
also responsible for the design of the fountain at
the entrance to the Hollywood Bowl (page 105)
and the panel above the front entrance to
Bullocks Wilshire department store (page 54).
The statuette was based on a design by Cedric
Gibbons, the Academy Award–winning movie
art director. In 1929 Gibbons designed an
early modern house in Santa Monica for his
wife, movie actress Dolores del Rio, the star of
Flying Down to Rio (1936). A one-time assistant to
Hugo Ballin (the prolific muralist and silent movie–director),
Gibbons later became the supervisory art director for
MGM, inheriting the position from the great French Art Deco
exponent Erté (Romain de Tirtoff). The artist had been brought to
Hollywood by movie mogul Louis B. Mayer, but finding it difficult to work
in the studio system, he left within a year, even though Mayer had

14

re-created Erté's Paris studio in Culver City, down to the smallest detail.

However, Erté's illustrations for *Harpers Bazaar* greatly influenced the work of the Hollywood movie designers, many of whom also worked in architecture and interior design, two prime examples being German émigrés under contract to Paramount Studios, Jock Peters (Bullocks Wilshire) and Ken Weber, the designer of the Disney Studio building, 1939–40.

Apart from the film industry, Los Angeles was rich in other commodities, primarily citrus and oil. Two of the city's great architectural edifices have long been lost to the wrecker's ball: the Sunkist (California Fruit Growers Exchange) Building and the magnificent Richfield Oil Building, whose bronze elevator doors now stand on Arco Plaza like tombstones in memory of this lost masterpiece (page 137). One must not dwell on their demise, however, as so much of Los Angeles's Art Deco heritage is left to appreciate.

Over the last quarter of a century I have discovered a rich vein of Art Deco running throughout L.A., which prompted my desire to record its jewels. In my photographs I decided to focus more on the decorative details of the city's buildings than on the buildings as a whole. The images in this book are a distillation from over four thousand photographs I have taken throughout Los Angeles County. Between the covers of this book the reader can enjoy in detail the vestiges of one of the most inspiring styles of the twentieth century.

—ARNOLD SCHWARTZMAN

TILE &

TERRAZZO

PREVIOUS SPREAD,
LEFT:
Glazed tile
drinking fountain,
Valentine School, 1937–38.
1650 Huntington Drive,
San Marino.
Norman Marsh,
David Smith, and
Herbert Powell.

PREVIOUS SPREAD,
RIGHT:
Terrazzo floor,
commercial building, 1930.
7290 Beverly Boulevard,
Los Angeles.
J. R. Horns.

THIS PAGE
AND OPPOSITE:
Tile murals,
Title Insurance & Trust
Company Building
and Annex, 1930.
419 (Annex) and
433 (Building)
S. Spring Street,
Los Angeles.
John Parkinson.

OPPOSITE:
Spanish-style ceramic tile,
Union Passenger Terminal,
1934–39.
800 N. Alameda Street,
Los Angeles.
John and Donald Parkinson,
J. H. Christie,
H. L. Gilman, R. J. Wirth.

THIS PAGE:
Glazed tile
drinking fountains,
Valentine School, 1937–38.
1650 Huntington Drive,
San Marino.
Norman Marsh,
David Smith, and
Herbert Powell.

TOP:
Glazed tiles over entrance,
Santa Monica City Hall,
1938–39.
1685 Main Street,
Santa Monica.
Donald B. Parkinson
and J. M. Estep.

CENTER AND BOTTOM:
Open terra-cotta
glazed tile grille,
Warner Building, 1927.
481 E. Colorado Boulevard,
Pasadena.
Marston and Maybury.

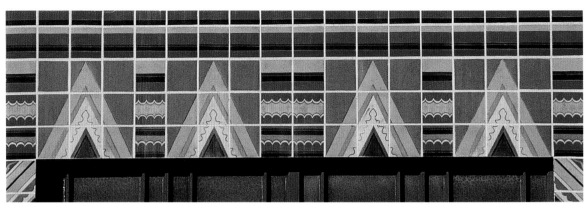

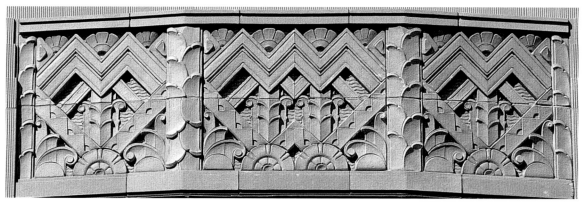

THIS PAGE:
Terra-cotta tile,
Warner Brothers
Western Theater,
now Wiltern Theater,
Pellissier Building,
1930–31.
3790 Wilshire
Boulevard,
Los Angeles.
Morgan, Walls,
and Clements.

THIS PAGE:
Catalina's indigenous tile, c. 1930, can be seen throughout the town of Avalon, Santa Catalina Island.

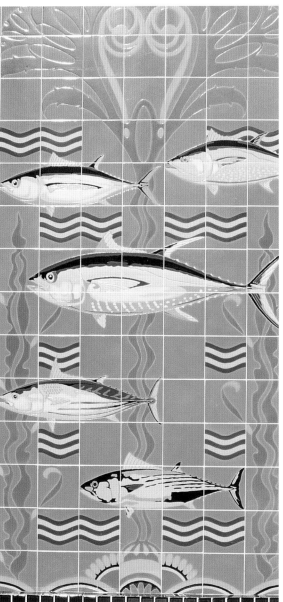

LEFT:
Entranceway mural detail, Casino Ballroom and Theater, 1928–29. 1 Casino Way, Avalon, Santa Catalina Island. Webber and Spaulding. Murals painted by John Gabriel Beckman. The murals were to be constructed of tile, but due to time constraints, they were painted. In 1986 this panel was finally created in tile by Stenton Wilcox under Beckman's supervision.

RIGHT:
Ceramic tile mural depicts the five species of tuna caught by the San Pedro fishing fleet and canned on Terminal Island. From top to bottom: bluefin, albacore, yellowfin, skipjack, and bonito. Created in Glendale by artisans of Gladding McBean and Company, 1934, for Van Camp Seafood Corporation, Tuna Street, Terminal Island. Moved to San Pedro Maritime Museum, 1989. Berth 84, Sixth Street, San Pedro.

THIS PAGE:
Green terra-cotta fish,
Burbank City Hall fountain,
1940–41. Olive Street,
Burbank.
William Allen and
George Lutzi.

THIS PAGE:
Facade and tiled screen detail, Burbank City Hall, 1940–41. Olive Avenue, Burbank.
William Allen and George Lutzi.

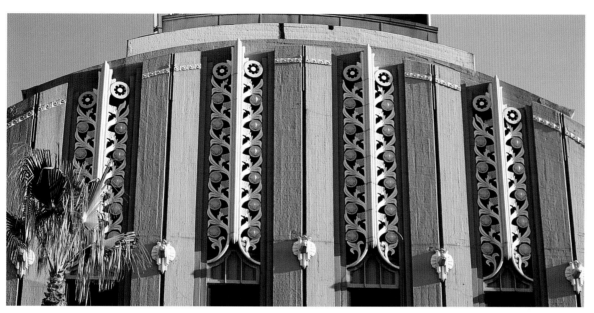

OPPOSITE:
Beverly Hills fountain, 1931.
Corner of Wilshire
and Santa Monica
Boulevards, Beverly Hills.
Designer:
Ralph C. Flewelling.
Sculptor: Merrell Gage.

TOP:
Kress and Company
Building, 1935.
6608 Hollywood Boulevard,
Hollywood.
Edward F. Sibbert.

BOTTOM:
Turquoise, gold, and yellow
glazed terra-cotta tiles,
J. J. Newberry Company
Building, the former
"five and dime" store,
1928.
6600 Hollywood Boulevard,
Hollywood.

LEFT:
Gold mosaic
quarter-cylinder and
black granite,
May Co. Department
Store building, 1940,
now part of the
Los Angeles County
Museum of Art.
6067 Wilshire Boulevard,
Los Angeles.
Albert C. Martin
and S. A. Marks.

RIGHT:
Glazed black and gold
terra-cotta tile,
Security First National
Bank of Los Angeles, 1929.
5209 Wilshire Boulevard,
Los Angeles.
Morgan, Walls,
and Clements.

OPPOSITE:
Glazed terra-cotta tiles,
Selik retail store, 1931.
273 S. Western Avenue,
Los Angeles.
Arthur E. Harvey.

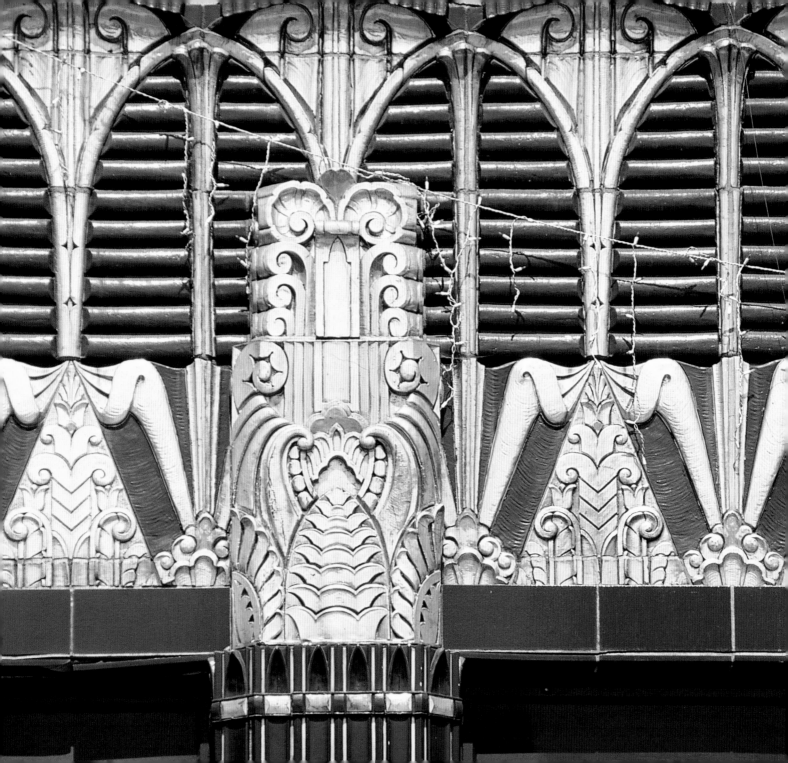

34

THIS PAGE:
Gold and turquoise glazed
terra-cotta tiles and gold
leaf (costing $25,000),
Eastern Columbia Building
facade details and lobby,
1930.
Built by self-made merchant
Adolph Sieroty as an
office and retail tower.
In 1930 the
Los Angeles Times
described the
terra-cotta facade as
"melting turquoise."
849 S. Broadway,
Los Angeles.
Claude Beelman.

36

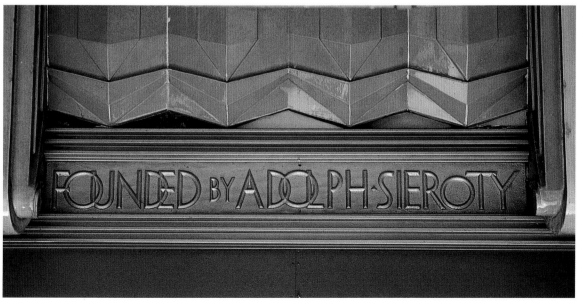

TOP:
Terra-cotta tile facade,
AND BOTTOM:
Lobby detail,
Eastern Columbia
Building, 1930.
849 S. Broadway,
Los Angeles.
Claude Beelman.

RIGHT:
The "Torch of Knowledge"
surmounts the glazed
tile roof,
Los Angeles Central
Library
Building, 1922–26.
630 W. Fifth Street,
Los Angeles.
Bertram G. Goodhue and
Carleton M. Winslow.
Sculpted figures:
Lee Lawrie.

OPPOSITE:
Clock Tower, Bay City
Guarantee and Loan
Association Building,
1929–30.
1225 Third Street,
Santa Monica.
Walker and Eisen.

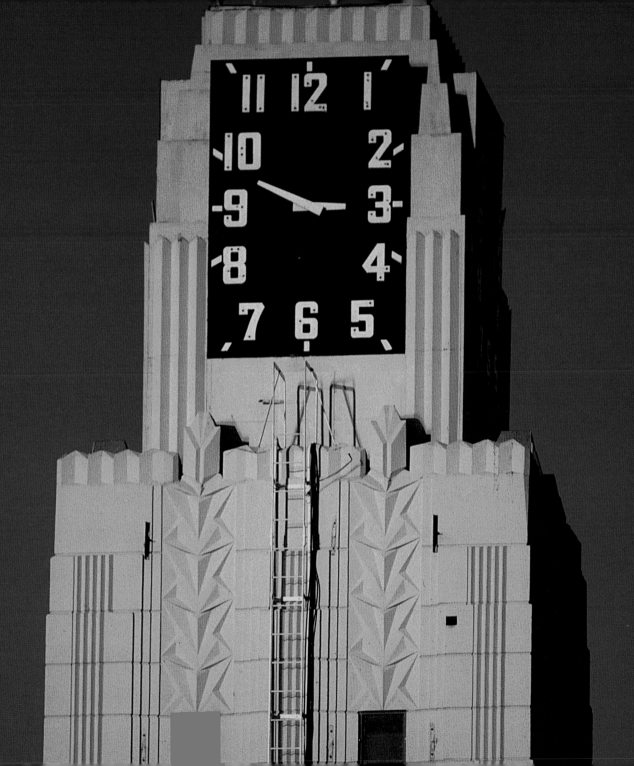

RIGHT
AND OPPOSITE:
Sidewalk terrazzo floor
medallions depicting
Los Angeles landmarks,
including City Hall,
Griffith Observatory,
the Coliseum, and the
Hollywood Bowl,
Clifton's Brookdale
Cafeteria, 1936.
648 S. Broadway,
Los Angeles.
Clifford Clifton.

OVERLEAF:
Entrance, Clifton's
Brookdale Cafeteria,
1936.
648 S. Broadway,
Los Angeles.
Clifford Clifton.

Terrazzo floors.

TOP LEFT:
S. Spring Street, Los Angeles.

TOP CENTER:
Fox/Bruin Theater, 1937.
926–940 Broxton Avenue,
Westwood.

TOP RIGHT:
Culver Theater, c. 1950.
Culver City.

CENTER LEFT:
Hollywood Theater, 1938.
Hollywood Boulevard,
Hollywood.

CENTER:
Reed Jewelers, c. 1929.
533 S. Broadway,
Los Angeles.

CENTER RIGHT:
Vine Theater, 1942.
6321 Hollywood Boulevard,
Hollywood.

BOTTOM LEFT:
Gordon Theater, 1936.
614 N. La Brea Avenue,
Los Angeles.

BOTTOM CENTER:
Alex Theater, 1939.
268 N. Brand Boulevard,
Glendale.

BOTTOM RIGHT:
El Rey Theater, c. 1928.
5515–5519 Wilshire
Boulevard, Los Angeles.

GLASS

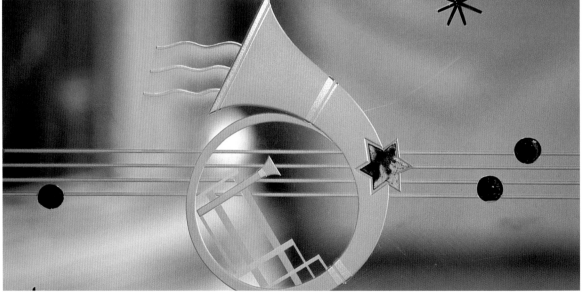

LEFT:
Neon sign,
Egyptian Theater, 1922.
6706 Hollywood Boulevard,
Hollywood.
Meyer and Holler.

RIGHT:
Neon sign,
El Rey Theater, c. 1928.
5515–5519 Wilshire
Boulevard, Los Angeles.
W. Clifford Balch.

TOP:
Neon marquee,
Fine Arts Theater, 1930s.
8556 Wilshire Boulevard,
Los Angeles.

BOTTOM:
Neon marquee,
Nuart Theater, 1930.
11272 Santa Monica
Boulevard, Los Angeles.

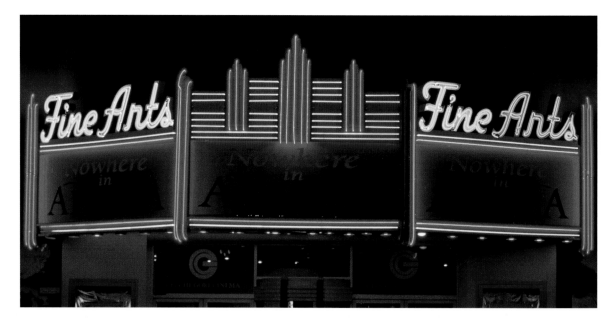

TOP:
Neon marquee,
Aero Theater,
Montana Avenue,
Santa Monica.
Built in 1939 by
the founder of
Douglas Aircraft Co.,
the theater was open
around the clock
for the benefit
of the employees.
Recently acquired
and restored by the
American Cinematheque.

BOTTOM:
Neon marquee,
Fox/Bruin Theater, 1937.
926–940 Broxton Avenue,
Westwood.
S. Charles Lee.

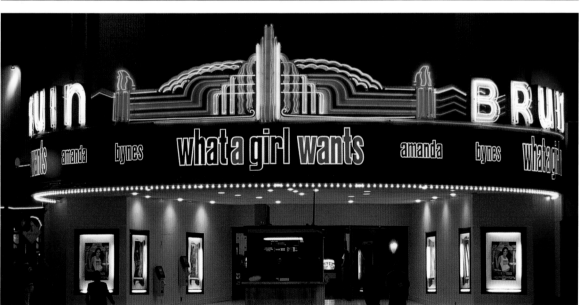

"TO BVILD A BVSINESS THAT WILL
NEVER KNOW COMPLETION

MADDUX

GRAF ZEPPELIN   D - LZ 127

PLASTER

PREVIOUS SPREAD,
LEFT:
Motto below sculpted
stone relief reads:
*"To build a business
that will never
know completion,"*
above main entrance,
Bullocks Wilshire
department store, 1928–29.
3050 Wilshire Boulevard,
Los Angeles.
John and Donald Parkinson;
Fell and Paradice;
Jock Peters.
Sculptor: George Stanley.

PREVIOUS SPREAD,
RIGHT:
"Speed of Transportation"
porte-cochère ceiling
frescoes by Herman Sachs,
Bullocks Wilshire
department store, 1928–29.
3050 Wilshire Boulevard,
Los Angeles.
John and Donald Parkinson;
Fell and Paradice;
Jock Peters.

RIGHT:
Alex Theater marquee,
1939.
268 N. Brand Boulevard,
Glendale.
Arthur G. Lindley and
Charles R. Selkirk.

TOP:
Fox/Bruin Theater, 1937.
926–940 Broxton Avenue,
Westwood.
S. Charles Lee.

BOTTOM:
Grauman's Chinese Theater,
1927.
6925 Hollywood Boulevard,
Hollywood.
Meyer and Holler.

LEFT:
Decorative column,
Grauman's Chinese Theater,
1927.
6925 Hollywood Boulevard,
Hollywood.
Meyer and Holler.

RIGHT:
Detail, Egyptian Theater,
1922.
Egyptian Revival style was
inspired by the discovery
of Tutankhamen's tomb
that same year.
6706 Hollywood Boulevard,
Hollywood.
Meyer and Holler.

OPPOSITE:
Cast concrete facade,
Mayan Theater, 1926–27.
1040 S. Hill Street,
Los Angeles.
Morgan, Walls,
and Clements.
Sculptor: Francisco Coneja.

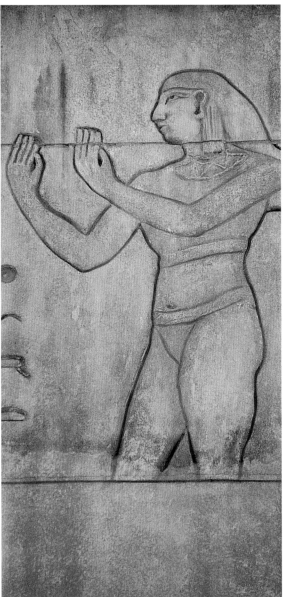

LEFT:
Academy Theater, 1939,
now a cathedral.
3100 Manchester
Boulevard, Inglewood.
S. Charles Lee.

RIGHT:
Loyola Theater, 1946,
now a church.
8610 S. Sepulveda
Boulevard, Los Angeles.
Clarence J. Smale.

OPPOSITE:
El Rey Theater, c. 1928.
5515–5519 Wilshire
Boulevard, Los Angeles.
W. Clifford Balch.

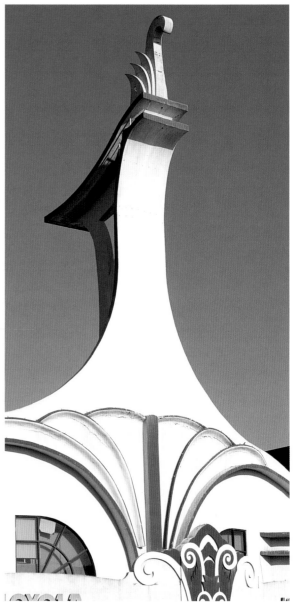

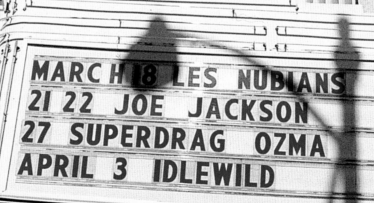

TOP LEFT:
St. Mary's Hospital,
1935–37.
10th Street, Long Beach.
J. E. Loveless.

TOP RIGHT:
Engine Company No. 1
Fire Station, 1940.
2230 Pasadena Avenue,
Los Angeles.

CENTER LEFT:
Venice Division
Police Station, 1930.
685 Venice Boulevard,
Venice.
Bureau of Construction.

CENTER RIGHT:
Long Beach Post Office and
Federal Building, 1931–32.
Third Street, Long Beach.
James A. Wetmore.

BOTTOM LEFT:
City of Pasadena
Municipal Light & Power
Dispatching Center,
c. 1936.
Pasadena.

BOTTOM RIGHT:
Department of Water
and Power building, 1935.
15345 Sunset Boulevard,
Pacific Palisades.
Frederick L. Roehrig.

PREVIOUS PAGE:
Los Angeles County/USC
Medical Center, 1928–33.
1200 N. State Street,
Los Angeles.
Edwin Bergstrom,
Myron Hunt,
Pierpont Davis,
Sumner P. Hunt, and
William Richards.

TOP:
Municipal Light, Water,
and Power, c. 1935.
2417 Daly Street,
Lincoln Heights.
S. Charles Lee.

BOTTOM:
Streamline Moderne
structure in
reinforced concrete,
Coca-Cola Bottling
Company, 1936–37.
1334 S. Central Avenue,
Los Angeles.
Robert V. Derrah.

OPPOSITE:
PWA-built
Municipal Ferry Building,
now a Maritime Museum,
1939–41.
Berth 84, Sixth Street,
San Pedro.

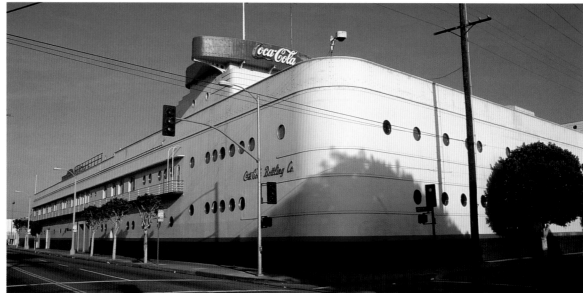

TOP:
South Pasadena
High School, 1937.
Fremont Avenue
and Lyndon Street,
South Pasadena.
Marsh, Smith, and Powell.

BOTTOM:
Long Beach Polytechnic
High School, 1932–36.
Atlantic and 15th Streets,
Long Beach.
Hugh R. Davies.

OPPOSITE:
Bank of America,
1934–35.
5620 Hollywood
Boulevard, Hollywood.

OPPOSITE:
Low-relief sculptured panels
(now covered),
formerly the Four Star Theater,
c. 1936, now a church.
5112 Wilshire Boulevard,
Los Angeles.
Walker & Eisen,
and C.A. Balch.

THIS PAGE:
Detail, stone relief balconies,
apartment building, 1930s.
511 S. Serrano Avenue,
Los Angeles.

THIS PAGE
AND OPPOSITE:
Cast concrete decoration,
Sunset Towers
Apartment Building, now
Argyle Hotel, 1929–31.
18358 Sunset Boulevard,
West Hollywood.
Leland A. Bryant.

TOP AND BOTTOM:
Cast concrete balconies,
Lafayette Hotel building,
1929.
Broadway and Linden
Avenues, Long Beach.
Schilling and Schilling.

OPPOSITE:
Hayworth Tower
apartment building, 1930s.
340 N. Hayworth Avenue,
Los Angeles.

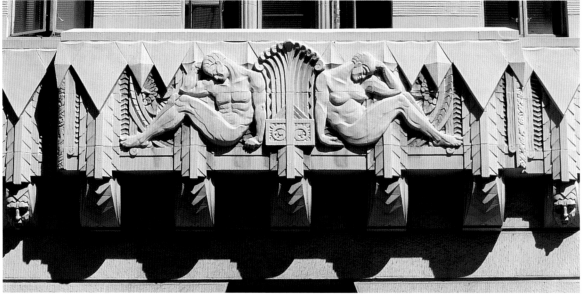

TOP:
Rooftop statuary,
AND BOTTOM:
Entrance, Val D'Amour
apartment building, 1928.
854 S. Oxford Avenue,
Los Angeles.
G. W. Power.

74

TOP LEFT:
Cast concrete crest,
Vandekamp's Holland
Dutch Bakery annex,
1930s.
Fletcher Drive, Los Angeles.

CENTER LEFT:
Cast concrete logo
for the former Don Lee
Cadillac dealership, 1929.
7005 Hollywood Boulevard,
Los Angeles.
Morgan, Walls,
and Clements.

BOTTOM LEFT:
Cast concrete medallion,
Helms Bakery building,
1930.
8800 Venice Boulevard,
Culver City.
E. L. Bruner.

RIGHT:
Arcadia News Journal
building, 1932.
53 Huntington Drive,
Arcadia.
Sculptor: J. J. Mora.

75

TOP:
Los Feliz Manor
apartment building, 1929.
4643 Los Feliz Boulevard,
Los Angeles.
Jack Grundfor.

BOTTOM:
Ravenwood Apartments,
c. 1928.
Mae West once occupied
a penthouse here.
570 N. Rossmore Avenue,
Hollywood.

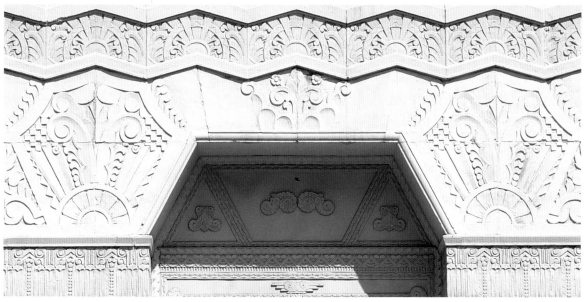

THIS PAGE:
Details, Assyrian-inspired
decoration,
Ravenwood Apartments,
c. 1928.
570 N. Rossmore Avenue,
Hollywood.

RIGHT:
Textured concrete blocks,
Sowden House, 1926.
5121 Franklin Avenue,
Los Angeles.
Lloyd Wright.

78

LEFT:
Apartment building, c. 1928.
Mansfield Avenue
and Third Street,
Los Angeles.

RIGHT:
Commercial building, 1930.
7290 Beverly Boulevard,
Los Angeles.
J. R. Horns.

RIGHT:
Marble window frame,
Max Factor Makeup
Salon, 1931.
1659–1666 Highland
Avenue, Hollywood.
S. Charles Lee.

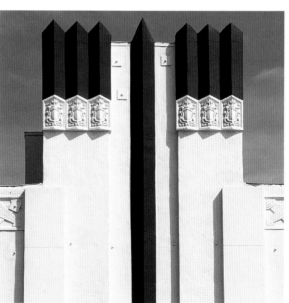

TOP LEFT:
Commercial building,
c. 1930.
8301 Beverly Boulevard,
Los Angeles.

BOTTOM LEFT:
Commercial building, 1929.
7223 Beverly Boulevard,
Los Angeles.
L. Mulgreen.

RIGHT:
Leimert Theater complex,
1931–32.
43rd Place, Leimert Park,
Los Angeles.
Morgan, Walls,
and Clements.

LEFT:
Entrance ceiling,
Warner Brothers
Western Theater,
now Wiltern Theater,
Pellissier Building, 1930–31.
3790 Wilshire Boulevard,
Los Angeles.
Morgan, Walls,
and Clements.

RIGHT:
Concrete decoration,
Fox–Warner Brothers
Theater, 1931.
478 W. Sixth Street,
San Pedro.
B. Marcus Priteca.

OPPOSITE:
Cast concrete panels,
commercial building,
c. 1928.
301 Wilshire Boulevard,
Santa Monica.

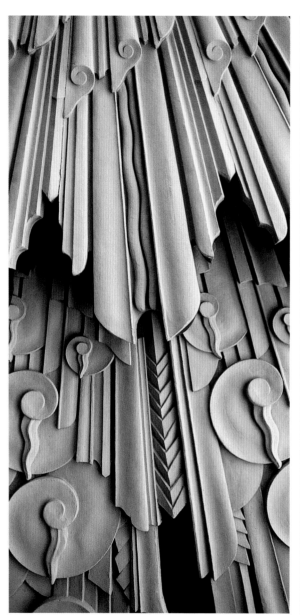

LEFT:
Cast concrete panel,
commercial building,
c. 1928.
1025 N. Sycamore Avenue,
Hollywood.

RIGHT:
Cast concrete panel,
commercial building,
c. 1930.
4813 Washington Boulevard,
Los Angeles.

TOP:
Cast concrete, exterior wall,
Paramount Studios, c. 1928.
5555 Melrose Avenue,
Hollywood.

BOTTOM:
Decorative stone panel,
Arcadia News Journal, 1932.
53 Huntington Drive,
Arcadia.
Sculptor: J. J. Mora.

THIS PAGE:
A variety of Art Deco
capitals, 1930s.
Los Angeles and
Long Beach.

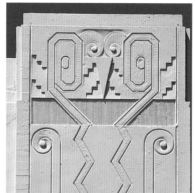

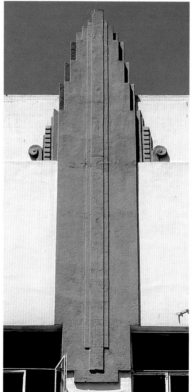

THIS PAGE:
Art Deco interpretations
of Corinthian capitals,
1930s.
Los Angeles.

OPPOSITE:
Cast concrete decoration,
Yucca-Vine Tower Building,
c. 1928.
Yucca Avenue,
Los Angeles.
Gogerty and Weyl.

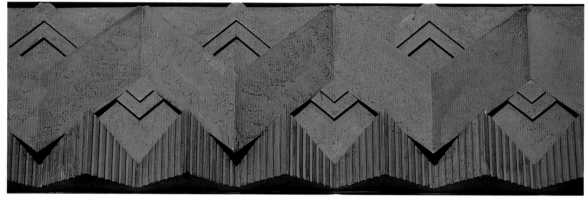

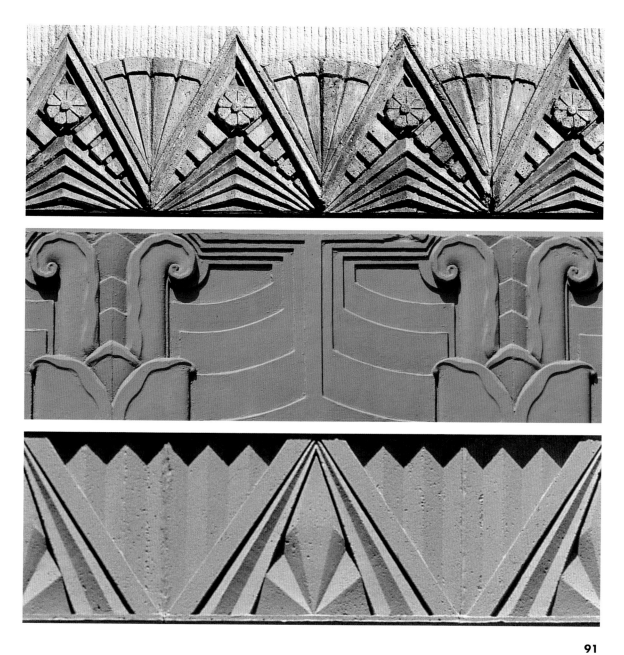

RIGHT:
Retail store, 1930s.
29 W. Colorado Boulevard,
Pasadena.

OPPOSITE:
Shop front, 1930s.
First Street, Long Beach.

TOP:
Decorative panel,
Dominguez-Wilshire
Building, 1930.
5410 Wilshire Boulevard,
Los Angeles.
Morgan, Walls,
and Clements.

BOTTOM:
Stone relief decoration,
commercial building,
1930s.
5505 Wilshire Boulevard,
Los Angeles.

OPPOSITE:
Entrance-way mural
details, Casino Ballroom
and Theater, 1928–29.
1 Casino Way, Avalon,
Santa Catalina Island.
Webber and Spaulding.
Murals:
John Gabriel Beckman.
The murals were to be
constructed of tile, but
only one was completed
in that material.
(see page 27)

THIS PAGE:
Two stone relief panels
above the entrance to
the U.S. Naval and Marine
Corps Reserve Center,
constructed by PWA,
1938–41.
Stadium Way, Los Angeles.
Robert Clements and
Associates.

OPPOSITE:
Terra-cotta figure
of Mercury,
Union Oil building, 1911,
remodeled 1930s.
215 W. Seventh Street,
Los Angeles.
John Parkinson and
Edwin Bergstrom.

TWO FIFTEEN

RIGHT
AND OPPOSITE:
Two surviving low-relief
sculpted panels from
the former site of
Tom Breneman's
restaurant, his
"Breakfast in Hollywood"
radio show, and the
American Broadcasting
Company, 1949.
1529–1559 N. Vine Street,
Hollywood.

THIS PAGE:
Goldleaf covered masks
of Tragedy and Comedy,
AND OPPOSITE:
Movietone crest, on
sound stage facades,
20th Century Fox Studio,
1930.
10201 W. Pico Boulevard,
Los Angeles.

LEFT:
Cast stone "Mercury"
holding a movie camera,
underside of fire escape,
TOP RIGHT:
Bas-relief side of fire escape,
BOTTOM RIGHT:
"Moses"
sculpted keystone,
AND OPPOSITE, TOP:
Figures above the entrance
depict directors,
producers, and architects,
OPPOSITE, BOTTOM:
Figures representing
drama, art, music,
and literature,
Hollywood–Western
Building, home of the
Motion Picture Producers
and Distributors of
America, Central Casting
and the Hays Office, 1928.
5500–5510 Hollywood
Boulevard, Hollywood.
S. Charles Lee.

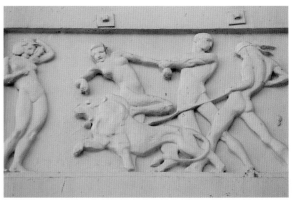

LEFT:
Statue in memory of
Rudolph Valentino, 1930.
DeLongpre Park,
DeLongpre Avenue,
Hollywood.
Sculptor: Roger Burnham.

Inscription reads:
*"Erected in memory
of Rudolph Valentino,
1895–1926, presented by
his friends and admirers
from every walk of life in
all parts of the world.
In appreciation of the
happiness brought to
them by his cinema
portrayals."*

RIGHT:
Cast concrete figure,
Wilshire Tower, 1929.
5514 Wilshire Boulevard,
Los Angeles.
Gilbert S. Underwood.

OPPOSITE:
Fountain, "Music,"
one of three sculpted
pieces representing music,
drama, and dance
at the entrance to the
Hollywood Bowl, 1935.
2310 N. Highland Avenue,
Los Angeles.
Sculptor: George Stanley.

RIGHT:
Decorative stone grilles,
Pantages Theater, 1929.
6233 Hollywood
Boulevard, Hollywood.
B. Marcus Priteca.
Decor:
Anthony Heinsbergen.

OPPOSITE:
One of several statues,
Pantages Theater, 1929.
6233 Hollywood Boulevard,
Hollywood.
B. Marcus Priteca.
Decor:
Anthony Heinsbergen.

RIGHT:
Copper-clad tower,
AND OPPOSITE:
Facade, Bullocks Wilshire
department store, 1928–29.
3050 Wilshire Boulevard,
Los Angeles.
John and Donald Parkinson;
Fell and Paradice;
Jock Peters.
Sculptor: George Stanley.

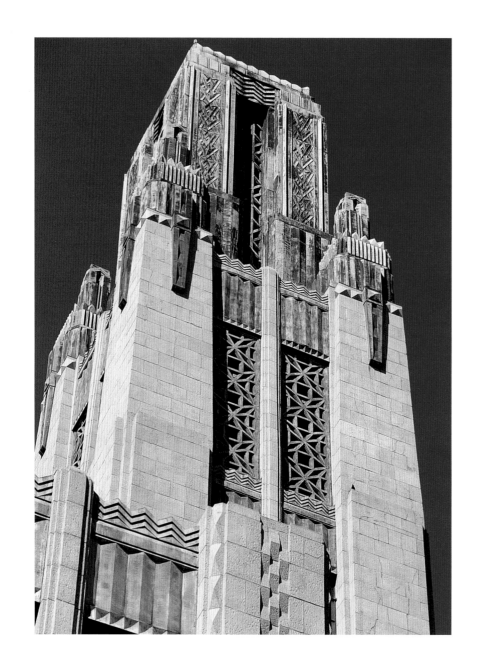

OPPOSITE:
Union Passenger
Terminal, 1934–39.
800 N. Alameda Street,
Los Angeles.
John and Donald Parkinson,
J. H. Christie,
H. L. Gilman, R. J. Wirth.

LEFT:
Crossroads of the World,
1936–37.
6671 W. Sunset Boulevard,
Hollywood.
Robert V. Derrah.

RIGHT:
Rooftop sign,
Dog and Cat Hospital, 1930s.
940 N. Highland Avenue,
Los Angeles.

OPPOSITE:
Commercial building,
1930s.
S. Vermont Avenue
and W. 81st Street,
Los Angeles.

THIS PAGE:
Columns sculpted by
Bartolo Mako depict
the school's motto:
"Achieve the Honorable,"
Hollywood High School
Science Building,
1934–35.
Sunset Boulevard and
Highland Avenue,
Los Angeles.
Marsh, Smith and Powell.

TOP LEFT AND RIGHT:
Relief sculptures,
San Pedro High School,
1935–37.
Leland Street, San Pedro.
Gordon B. Kaufmann.

BOTTOM:
One of three cast
concrete bas-relief panels,
Venice High School,
1935–37.
13000 Venice Boulevard,
Venice.

OPPOSITE:
Curved relief panel
"Pageant of Education"
by Bartolo Mako,
Lou Henry Hoover School,
1938.
Camilla Street, Whittier.
William H. Harrison.

LOU HENRY HOOVER SCHOOL

CLASES DE INGLES
PARA ADULTOS
FREE ENGLISH CLASSES FOR ADULTS
GUARDERIA REGISTRACION
GRATIS DIARIA
REGISTER ANYTIME 562 789-3150
WHITTIER CITY SCHOOL DISTRICT
COMMUNITY BASED ENGLISH TUTORING (CBET) PROGRAM

WHAT YOU WOULD HAVE IN THE LIFE OF A NATION
YOU MUST FIRST PUT INTO ITS SCHOOLS
VON HUMBOLT

THIS PAGE:
Stone relief frieze
depicting transportation,
commercial building,
c. 1936.
2121 San Fernando Road,
Glassel Park, Los Angeles.

OPPOSITE, TOP:
WPA/Bureau of
Construction–built
exposed concrete relief
sculpture, Venice Police
and Fire Station, 1930.
685 Venice Boulevard,
Venice.

OPPOSITE, CENTER:
WPA bas-relief by
Bartolo Mako,
Burbank City Hall,
1940–41.
Olive Street, Burbank.
William Allen and
George Lutzi.

OPPOSITE, BOTTOM:
Bas-relief,
I. Magnin & Company
building, 1938–39.
3240 Wilshire Boulevard,
Los Angeles.
Myron Hunt and
H. C. Chambers.

116

M.ROSANDICH

THIS PAGE:
Cast concrete decorative medallions,
Walker Building (originally Martis Department Store),
1929.
401 Pine Avenue,
Long Beach.
Meyer and Holler.

OPPOSITE:
Intaglio marble facade,
Reed Jewelers, c. 1929.
533 S. Broadway,
Los Angeles.

RIGHT:
"Hydro-electric Energy,"
one of three relief panels
by Merrell Gage, the
other two representing
light and power,
Southern California
Edison Building, 1930–34.
601 W. Fifth Street,
Los Angeles.
Allison and Allison
(Austin Whittlesey).

WILSHIRE TOWER

LEFT:
Stone intaglio panel
above the entrance
to Desmonds
department store,
Wilshire Tower,
1929.
5514 Wilshire Boulevard,
Los Angeles.
Gilbert S. Underwood.

LEFT:
Cast stone eagle,
entranceway to
Burbank City Hall,
1940–41.
Olive Avenue, Burbank.
William Allen and
George Lutzi.

TOP CENTER
AND RIGHT:
Stylized sculpted eagles,
National Trust and
Savings Building, 1935.
Philadelphia Street and
Greenleaf Avenue,
Whittier.
William H. Harrison.

CENTER:
Sculpted eagle,
commercial building, 1929.
5505 Wilshire Boulevard,
Los Angeles.
Frank Rasche.

BOTTOM:
Plaster eagle,
commercial building,
1930s.
2745 Manchester Boulevard,
Los Angeles.

OPPOSITE:
California Bank building,
c. 1930.
9441 Wilshire Boulevard,
Beverly Hills.

BURBANK
CITY HALL

MAYOR
FRANK C TILLSON

COUNCILMEN
WALTER R. HINTON
ELMER J JACKSON
JAMES T. LAPSLEY
ERNEST R ROTHE

CITY ENGINEER
HOWARD E STITES

ARCHITECTS:
WILLIAM ALLEN
W GEORGE LUTZI

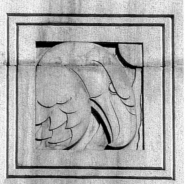

TOP:
Three stone
carved eagles,
AND BOTTOM:
Stone cast
relief panel above
the entrance,
Los Angeles Branch,
Federal Reserve Bank
of San Francisco, 1930.
S. Olive Street, Los Angeles.
John and Donald Parkinson.
Sculptor: Edgar Walter.

LEFT:
Sculpted eagles,
Department of
Water and Power,
Station 10,
City of Los Angeles,
c. 1930.
6776 Hawthorn Avenue,
Hollywood.

& WOOD

PREVIOUS SPREAD,
LEFT:
Metal entrance arch
detail, Valentine School,
1937–38.
1650 Huntington Drive,
San Marino.
Norman Marsh,
David Smith, and
Herbert Powell.

PREVIOUS SPREAD,
RIGHT:
Parking/Exit sign,
Ambassador Hotel, 1921
(entranceway added later).
3400 Wilshire Boulevard,
Los Angeles.
Myron Hunt.

TOP:
PWA bronze eagle above
the entrance,
U.S. Customs House and
Post Office, 1935.
Beacon Street, San Pedro.

BOTTOM:
Metal grille above
the entrance,
U.S. Post Office, 1930s.
4201 E. Imperial Highway,
Los Angeles.

OPPOSITE:
Bronze eagle over
entrance to
Federal Building, 1938–40.
S. Spring and
W. Temple Streets,
Los Angeles.
Louis A. Simon.

THIS PAGE
AND OPPOSITE:
Five of twelve bronze
panels above the main
entrance depict the various
topics covered by the
Los Angeles Times.
Times Mirror Building,
1931–35.
First and S. Spring Streets,
Los Angeles.
Gordon Kaufmann.

OIL

RIGHT:
Decorative metal
window grille,
Federal Building,
1938–40.
S. Spring and
W. Temple Streets,
Los Angeles.
Louis A. Simon.

LEFT:
Metal window grille,
Dominguez-Wilshire
Building, 1930.
5410 Wilshire Boulevard,
Los Angeles.
Morgan, Walls,
and Clements.

RIGHT:
Metal window grille,
Producers Film Center,
c. 1928.
Former offices of
Howard Hughes.
Romaine Street and
N. Sycamore Avenue,
Hollywood.
Otto K. Olsen.

RIGHT:
Metal entrance arch,
Valentine School,
1937–38.
1650 Huntington Drive,
San Marino.
Norman Marsh,
David Smith, and
Herbert Powell.

134

THIS PAGE:
Metal railing and gates,
with alphabet
and numerals,
Valentine School,
1937–38.
1650 Huntington Drive,
San Marino.
Norman Marsh,
David Smith, and
Herbert Powell.

Stainless steel and enamel
exterior murals by
Millard Sheets.

TOP LEFT AND BOTTOM:
Murals illustrate
California history,
AND TOP RIGHT:
State of Texas history.
Mark Keppel High School,
1939.
501 E. Hellman Avenue,
Alhambra.
Marston and Maybury.

OPPOSITE:
Bronze elevator doors
from the Richfield Oil
Building,1929,
demolished in 1968.
Morgan, Walls,
and Clements.

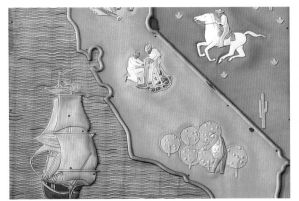

RIGHT:
Mailbox,
Oviatt Building,1927–28.
617 S. Olive Street,
Los Angeles.
Walker and Eisen.

OPPOSITE:
Metal gate,
Oviatt Building, 1927–28.
617 S. Olive Street,
Los Angeles.
Walker and Eisen.

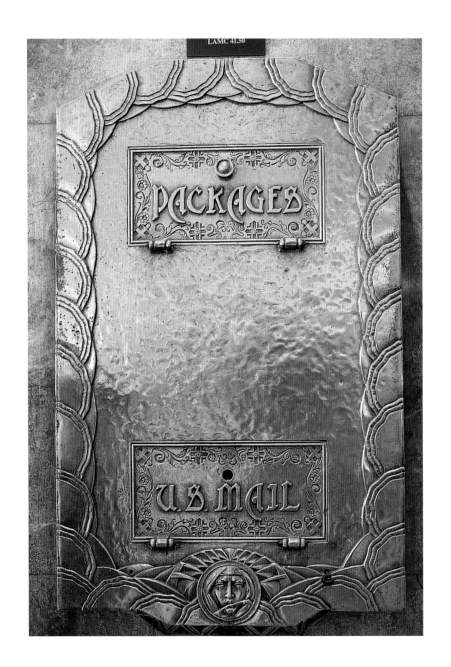

RIGHT:
Rear garage
entrance gates,
Sunset Towers
Apartment Building,
now Argyle Hotel,
1929–31.
8358 Sunset Boulevard,
Los Angeles.
Leland A. Bryant.

OPPOSITE:
Metal gates,
Banks-Huntley building,
1929–31.
634 S. Spring Street,
Los Angeles.
John and Donald Parkinson.

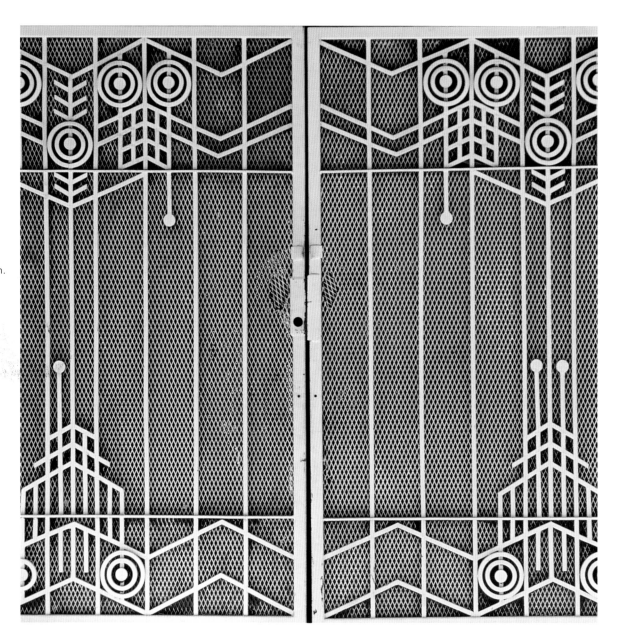

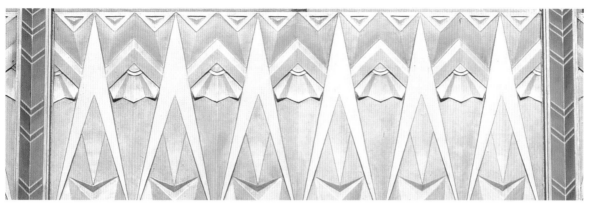

OPPOSITE:
Cast iron grille,
Pantages Theater, 1929.
6233 Hollywood
Boulevard,
Hollywood.
B. Marcus Priteca.
Decor:
Anthony Heinsbergen.

THIS PAGE:
Decorative metal panels.

TOP:
Security First National
Bank of Los Angeles, 1929.
5209 Wilshire Boulevard,
Los Angeles.
Morgan, Walls,
and Clements.

CENTER AND BOTTOM:
William Fox building,
c. 1929.
608 S. Hill Street,
Los Angeles.
S. Tilden Norton.

THIS PAGE:
Window grilles,
music store, 1920s.
California Boulevard,
Glendale.

OPPOSITE, TOP:
Steel sheeting decoration,
Grandstand rear facade,
AND BOTTOM:
Club House,
Santa Anita Racetrack,
1935.
Arcadia.
Gordon B. Kaufmann.

LEFT:
Detail, box office panel,
Warner Brothers
Western Theater,
now Wiltern Theater,
Pellissier Building, 1930–31.
3790 Wilshire Boulevard,
Los Angeles.
Morgan, Walls,
and Clements.

RIGHT TOP:
Bronze medallion,
Burbank City Hall,
1940–41.
Olive Street, Burbank.
William Allen and
George Lutzi.

RIGHT BOTTOM:
Decorative grilles,
commercial building,
c. 1930.
Westwood Boulevard
and Weyburn Avenue,
Westwood.

LEFT:
Brass ventilation grille,
Southern California
Edison Building, 1930–34.
601 W. Fifth Street,
Los Angeles.
Allison and Allison
(Austin Whittlesey).

OPPOSITE:
Copper plaque, 1930s.
Premiere Towers
apartment building.
621–625 S. Spring Street,
Los Angeles.

LEFT:
Three of six bronze
door panels based on
Greek mythology,
First Class Dining Salon,
Queen Mary, 1934.
1126 Queens Highway,
Long Beach.
Sculptors:
Walter and Donald Gilbert.

RIGHT:
Bronze and frosted
glass door panel.
Queen Mary, 1934.

TOP LEFT
AND BOTTOM LEFT:
White metal alloy
balustrades,
Queen Mary, 1934.
Sculptor and designer:
Austin Crompton Roberts.

TOP RIGHT:
Metal ventilation grille,
Verandah Grill,
Queen Mary, 1934.

BOTTOM RIGHT
AND OPPOSITE:
Metal ventilation grille,
Observation Lounge,
Queen Mary, 1934.
1126 Queens Highway,
Long Beach.

LEFT:
Metal tower,
Roxie Theater, 1931–32.
518 S. Broadway,
Los Angeles.
John M. Cooper.

RIGHT:
Metal tower,
Beacon Laundry, 1930s.
Washington Boulevard,
Culver City.

OPPOSITE:
Roof top sign, Broadway
department store, 1931.
6300 Hollywood
Boulevard, Hollywood.

TOP:
Thomas Jefferson
High School auditorium,
1936.
E. 41st Street,
Los Angeles.
Stiles O'Clements.

CENTER:
Metal street number,
Engine Company No. 1
Fire Station, 1940.
2230 Pasadena Avenue,
Los Angeles.

BOTTOM:
Buffum's Autoport, 1941.
123 W. First Street,
Long Beach.
Engineer: J. H. Davis.

OVERLEAF:
Brass signs at entrance
to Story Building garage,
1934.
Sixth Street, Los Angeles.
Morgan, Walls,
and Clements.